WARREN INSPIRE RYAN

THE ART OF
BEING
Yourself

WARREN INSPIRE RYAN

THE ART OF
BEING
Yourself

It starts with saying 'I got this'

For my brother, Matthew. My biggest inspiration, known for his loving heart and being an amazing father to his two beautiful children, Kaylon and Pixie.

Contents

Preface

Warren Inspire is not your typical motivational speaker. He is a strategist that gives people solutions to their problems to give them the edge in their personal life and in business. In the space of eight years, Warren has travelled the world as an international speaker and confidence coach, giving people the tools to be themselves in any situation. Warren's self-development journey started when his hopes of becoming a professional football player ended and Warren found himself depressed and at rock bottom. This was the catalyst for Warren gaining this philosophy and transforming his life, which started by understanding the psychology of the mind. How the mind works and how you can change existing beliefs and create new ones is what underpins his 21 Day Mind and Body Program that hundreds of people have already completed, changing their lives for the better.

During the COVID-19 pandemic, Warren founded the Got This Movement which is a "Netflix" style platform for self-development. Everything you need to help develop yourself in one place. The aim is to make changing your life as easy as choosing which TV programme to watch.

SELF-CONFIDENCE IS WHAT I THRIVE ON.

I AM DETERMINED TO FOLLOW THROUGH UNTIL FINISHED.

———————————

Chapter 1: The Commitment

Here's the thing about books: a lot of people pick them up and read a couple of pages before putting them back on the shelf again to collect dust. This is called 'shelf-development' not self-development. I, myself, have been guilty of doing this in the past.

But this is more than a book. This is a manual that is going to help you change your life for the better. I want to begin with you making a commitment to yourself that when you pick this book up and start reading it, you're going to finish it. Will you agree to make that commitment and come on this journey with me? If you can promise me that you will finish the book, then I can promise you that your life will never be the same again. Deal?

I have spent the past 10 years of my life on a personal development journey, the same journey that you are currently on or are about to start. My journey started with me feeling like I was stuck, like there was some kind of void in my life and like I was at a crossroads. I have studied personal development, psychology, the mind, and the body religiously. I have come across so much incredible knowledge and information that has ultimately changed my life. I've read so many books, listened to different mentors and attended numerous events. I've put everything that I have learnt into practice and have got real-life results, allowing me to create the philosophies and strategies that you are going to discover in this book. What took me 10 years is going to take you a fraction of the time.

I am promising that if you read this book and you take action, you are going to get results. You are going to have the ability to manage your emotions effectively, to communicate effectively, and understand how your mind works so that you can create a life that you love. You are here because you know that you deserve more than a life of only having what you need to get by or survive. You are here and you know there is a better way of living that you deserve.

Before I get into my philosophies and teachings, which will be the main part of this book, I want to give a little bit of background information about what got me to this point in my life. I wish for you to gain a better understanding of the highs and lows of my journey so that you know how much my life has changed, simply from the very practices I am about to teach you.

I grew up in a city called Oxford, which is famously known for its prestigious university, boat races, and centuries-old traditions. It is also known for being a very wealthy town with million-pound mansions and five-star restaurants. However, this was not the life that I knew. I grew up on an estate called Blackbird Leys, which is known for its prominence of criminal behaviour, drugs, and gang violence.

My mother had me when she was 17 years old, still just a child herself. She was learning to be a mum for the first time, completely alone. While she was raising me, she became involved with a lot of very abusive men and endured a lot of violence. As a child, I witnessed all of it and experienced this domestic violence as a part of my everyday home life. It deeply affected me, making me shy and closed off. All I wanted was to protect my mum. As I got older, she became addicted to drugs. It started out with cannabis but, over time, it turned into the frequent use of class-A drugs like crack cocaine and heroin. From such a young age I saw the drugs change her; she stopped being a mother and she became a slave to these substances, and all I could do was watch it. I saw her self-sabotage in front of my eyes, and it resulted in me and my siblings being taken into foster care.

This neglect alongside my experiences of growing up in foster care made me feel so different to everyone else my age, when really all I wanted was to be loved and seen as 'normal'. As a result of this, during my time in foster care, I learnt how to mirror and how to mask how I was actually feeling. I knew even at my young age that I did not want anyone to feel sorry for me or to treat me differently. I spent years believing I was broken and trying to fit in.

When I was 13 years old, my mum went to rehab and turned her life around. She then won a court

case to get us all back together again as a family. It was the best time of my life, being back with her and my siblings again, but I was still on this people-pleasing mission that began while I was in care.

I still had this deeply-ingrained fear of being treated like I was different. I wanted to prove to people that I was just the same as everybody else despite what had happened in my short life. However, in me doing that I lost my gift, my identity, the thing that made me 'me'.

I threw myself into my life-long passion which was football. I was at a club called Bristol Rovers playing at a youth level – football was my whole life. I was one step away from my dream of being a professional footballer. Then at 19 years old, I was released, and suddenly my dream and everything that I claimed significance for was taken away from me. I had a complete lack of purpose. This was what triggered me to spiral into depression. Everything I had suppressed throughout my entire childhood came out all at once, and this is when I went through one of the lowest times of my life. I felt lost, I felt broken, I felt alone. I couldn't see any point in going on.

I became suicidal and I started to have thoughts of not wanting to be here any longer. I will never

forget how that felt. I went to see a doctor and I told her what I had been going through and the emotions that I was experiencing. She was the first person I had opened up to. In my naive mind at the time, I think I was expecting her to give me a big hug and tell me that everything was going to be okay. I think we all feel that with the first person we truly confide in; we just want them to comfort us. Of course, she didn't do that. Instead, she prescribed me anti-depressants. I felt so alone at that moment and I did not want to take medication. I had experienced such a negative connection with drugs throughout my life, seeing what my mum had gone through. I feared becoming dependent on them and so I was adamant on finding a holistic way of overcoming this depression.

At that time, completely out of the blue, something happened that changed my life forever. Now that I look back, I realise that this was fate. I received a phone call; it was about a position I had applied for to coach football in the USA. I knew when I applied that I did not have the qualifications I needed to get the position, so I had not hoped for much. However, when I answered the phone, I was told that someone had dropped out at the very last minute and I was offered the job. Without any hesitation, I said yes. I looked up to the sky and I knew it was a sign, so I put the phone down, went to the US embassy, got my visa, and used all of the money in my bank account for a ticket to the States. I flew out there for the job, and while I was living there, my journey to self-discovery began. It started when I came across a video by a motivational speaker named Eric Thomas and realised that he had an identical upbringing to mine. There I was, feeling sorry for myself and asking the world, 'Why me?' when there was this man with the same past as me, but he was on a stage speaking to thousands of people and telling them things that I thought you couldn't tell anyone, things that I thought you had to keep to yourself.

In that moment, it was like a penny had dropped, and I realised that I had missed something huge. This entire time I had been so wrapped up in my own feelings that I had not been able to see that my story could help others. That's when I made the commitment to myself that I was going to take note of this journey to self-discovery and keep track of it so that I could help other people. I had found my purpose.

My first step was when I made a commitment to myself that I was going to impact one million lives in five years. I did not know how I was going to achieve this huge goal because I did not have a lot of self-confidence at the time. What I did know was that I was going to do it. I had a reason now, and it gave me a sense of purpose that would later become my 'Why', which I will get into later.

This purpose burned inside of me and I knew that I just had to do it. If I could help other people that are going through what I have, if I could be their hope, then it would make sense of all of the trauma and pain that I had experienced in my life. This is the moment when I went from being a victim to being a teacher. Having that 'Why' of helping other people, gave me all the motivation I needed to work on myself. You can't give what you haven't got. I started studying psychology and the mind and I came across more speakers and mentors, such as Tony Robbins, Jim Rohn, Zig Ziglar, and Les Brown. These mentors taught me the theory but it was the action I took that got the results. They were always talking about the same thing: mindset. I studied how the mind worked so that I could finally get in the driver's seat of my mind and I quickly learnt that the person I thought I was, wasn't actually me. This identity that I had constructed for myself was nothing more than a bunch of beliefs that I had learnt through my experiences in life. This is the same for everyone. We are who we believe we are based on what we have been told by our parents, through the schooling system, through the things that we have been exposed to. When you realise this fact, it gives you the freedom and the ability to create the person you have always wanted to be. I was realising that you can literally write down the characteristics and personality that you want to have on a piece of paper and then get to work on creating those beliefs. So that is exactly what I did.

I learnt the ability to create a new perception of the world, but more importantly of myself. The quality of life that we have is a reflection of how we feel about ourselves and we live the life we believe we deserve. A lot of us have a perception of ourselves that was created when we were children but that is carried with us through our adult lives. What we need to do is differentiate between what has happened to us and who we are. As adults, we must see the things that we have gone through and understand that we were not to blame for those things. We must learn to remove those labels that society has put on us.

When I studied this, I knew knowledge alone wasn't enough. I needed to immerse myself entirely into this way of living. It's a bit like learning how to swim in that way: you can read all of the books in the world about swimming but if you want to actually learn how to swim, you have to get into the pool. You are not going to be great at something right away, but the more you do it the better you get. For example, I knew that if I wanted to help others by sharing this philosophy that I was learning, I had to communicate effectively. I was insecure and shy, so I knew I wasn't going to be the best speaker at the beginning and that I was going to make loads of mistakes. I knew I was going to be laughed at and judged. To overcome this, I simply referred back to my reason for wanting to do this, my 'Why'. I knew that if I could help somebody to overcome the pain that they were going through, then that makes it all worth it. I was willing to be laughed at and I was willing to be judged if it meant that I could help someone.

I went about creating the new beliefs that I knew I needed to get where I was going. I reconditioned my mind, which allowed me to remove the ego-based fear – the fear that prevents people from being themselves. I became confident, and when

I say confident, I mean being the person that you are behind closed doors in public. I could finally take the mask off and be the authentic me, who did not need the external approval that so many of us feel like we need. Once I learnt how to manage my mind, I could speak on a stage in front of thousands of people without even breaking a sweat. To share the strategies I had learnt, I launched my own coaching business called the 'Fearless Speaking Academy', working with business owners, teachers, and students and teaching them how to speak fearlessly on stage. I then created the 'I Can Make You Confident in a Day' event across Europe, which helped people who wanted to be more confident. In my personal life, I had created my own family, with my partner at the time and my son, Noah, living in London. The vision that I had written down had become my reality.

I really was living a life that I loved as a result of truly being myself. Then, just when I thought I had it all sussed, life, as it does for everyone in some way or another, threw another challenge my way. You see, understanding how to manage the mind is one thing, but if you stop working on it, then you can lose control again. I went through a devastating break-up with the mother of my son and this triggered me. All of my trauma from growing up with a broken family came up at once. The thought of not being with my son full-time was crushing. It stopped me in my tracks, I stopped doing the work that I had devoted myself to. I stopped doing my morning routine and generally taking care of myself. I buried my head in the sand and quickly spiralled back into depression. I remember feeling so lost and asking myself how this could have happened. I could not fathom how, after all of my work, I had ended up right back where I had started. But the reason was clear, I had stopped implementing all the strategies I had learnt and the mind is like a muscle – it requires constant effort to remain strong.

And then, when I did not think things could get any worse, I lost my younger brother. It was and still is to this day the most traumatic and devastating thing that has happened in my life. We were so incredibly close growing up; we only really had each other at times. During those dark days, I felt like there was no point anymore, that no matter what personal development I did, it would not help me to overcome this. Part of my life had ended. It was at this point that I started to completely self-sabotage. I had come back to that same feeling as I did at 19 years old. I did not want to be here anymore. I started doing things that would harm my body, I just didn't care. I wanted it to give up on me so that I would not have to feel this intense pain anymore.

This part of my life brings me to a time that I am sure every single person reading this can relate to in one way or another: in March 2020, the world was plunged into uncertainty during the outbreak of COVID-19. A global pandemic was announced, and then lockdown. New territory for everybody and no indication of what we were supposed to do other than stay at home. For many people, the pandemic was a catalyst for mental downfall, but for me, it proved to be the opposite. Being in lockdown, I found myself with more time to think than I had ever had in my life and, without even meaning to, I began self-reflecting again. I had a lot of time to work on myself, and what I realised was that even more so than before, a lot of people out there were going through extreme pain.

One morning, I remember waking up and feeling that something had to change. I looked at myself and said aloud, 'I got this', and I wholeheartedly meant it. That morning was like a sign that I was going to help others to get back up, no matter what they were going through. For those who had lost people, I wanted to give them the will to live on, and that was going to be my motivation to get back on my feet again. Going through all of that is what has created the book that you are holding right now. I do not know what tomorrow brings, but if I can share this philosophy and my story, if I can help one person by writing this book, it will make it all worth it.

This book is also a dedication to my brother, Matthew. He was my biggest inspiration growing up; he was fearless, he was confident, he was not scared to ask for anything or to speak to anyone. He made me realise that I wanted to have a voice.

I did not have a voice as a kid; I was shy and scared of everything. So, this book is for him, Matthew Ryan. His name will live on for as long as I do and long after that.

This is my gift to you. That is why I do not want you to put this book down and never come back to it. I want you to read this book front to back. I am going to share what I know to help you achieve the life that you know you deserve.

AS I GROW MORE
CONNECTED TO MY SOUL,
MY LIFE'S PURPOSE
BECOMES CLEARER AND
CLEARER.

Chapter 2: The 'Why'

Changing your life is not easy. In fact, it is probably the hardest thing you are ever going to do. However, something I know for sure is that if you have a powerful, emotional reason to do what you are doing, and that reason is bigger than any fear or comfort you have, then you will overcome your fears and do it anyway. This is what I call the 'Why' – it is the reason 'why' you are doing what you have set out to do.

Your 'Why' has got to have emotion attached to it. It is your emotional 'Why' that gets you up before your alarm clock, that gets you to do things you don't want to do, things you put off, the things that scare you. If you're like me, and you've had things happen that were beyond your control, if you're sick and tired of being sick and tired, if you are ready to change your life, then you need a reason for doing it. When we are depressed or down, we do not care about ourselves, so of course, we can give up on ourselves. The power of a strong, emotional 'Why', however, is that you're not just doing this for yourself, you're doing it for a reason that is bigger than you. It needs to be something that is big enough to get you out of bed each morning, no questions asked.

That is the power behind the 'Why'. It has got to be attached to something so huge that you cannot help but go out and do it. That is why you are going to put the work in, that is why you are going to make it happen – because your 'Why' depends on it. It needs to be something that's very close to your heart: your children, your parents, your friends, your local community, or, most importantly, the reason why you are here. I have heard Wayne Dyer say, 'We are souls having a human experience' meaning there is a deeper reason for our existence. A huge part of creating an effective 'Why' is deciding to contribute to a cause that is bigger than ourselves and our lives. So, if you have been through something, for example, if you have gone through depression and you want to help people that are going through depression, that is a cause.

I want you to write down below why you are doing this. This book is not just about reading, it's about taking action, and this is your first task. I want you to write down all of the reasons why you want to achieve your goals. Every single person and reason that you are doing this for. Get so emotionally invested in your 'Why' that it gives you no choice but to do it.

I want you to write down your answers to these questions:

Why do you need to have a change in your life?

Stop procrastination, "Suzy" needs me

What are you sick and tired of?

Being unhealthy, lied to, not loving myself enough.

What are you ready to overcome in your life?

Fear, past failures.

Who are you inspiring? *My family, friends*

Those struggling with their weight and health

What is going to stop you from quitting?

NOTHING

What is your 'Why? *Legacy, change others lives who are struggling with self doubt*

self sabotage, self hate - for self love

One thing that helped me maintain the focus on my 'Why' was to journal all of this online. Social media is a platform that can reach thousands, if not millions of people, so when I journaled my story of overcoming what I had been through and creating this life of living on my terms, that is how I shared it. I told people where I was in life, what my mission was, and how I was going to get there. The thing about sharing your journey is that people are seeing you and you end up becoming a voice of inspiration for them. My inbox soon became full of messages from people I didn't even realise were seeing my posts. They end up believing in themselves because they see someone going through the same thing they are going through, and you are showing them what is possible. This holds you accountable, which is such a powerful thing about sharing our stories – we end up doing it to help others. Doing it on social media means you are going to impact so many people's lives, some who are close to you and some whom you will never even know you are helping. It gives a whole new meaning to your life. Even if your story helps one person, you have made a difference.

Your 'Why' is going to be the reason for you to achieve what you want to in life without giving up. Applying this philosophy is going to change your life. It is going to give you a life that you love. How are you going to feel when you live that life without the boundaries or limitations that you put on yourself? How are you going to feel when you learn to love yourself? What is your life going to look like? What's your family's life going to look like? What is your contribution? Who do you want to help? Whose voice do you want to be and how do you plan on doing it? Your power lies in recognising how much you can help others. As author Rob Brown says, 'If you can speak, you can influence, and if you can influence, you can change lives'.

THE MIND IS YOUR TOOL. LEARN TO BE ITS MASTER AND NOT ITS SLAVE.

Chapter 3: The Mind

What is the mind? When you picture the mind, what do you think of? Some say a lightbulb, others say a brain – it's different for everyone. Regardless of which visual comes to mind, it tends to be a very abstract image that people think of – picturing a brain or a lightbulb doesn't really mean anything – and it certainly doesn't help with our understanding of the mind.

What if I told you that I have something to replace that meaningless image? Something that you can picture when thinking of the mind that will help you change your mindset and eventually change your life?

A while back, I watched a video by Bob Proctor where he explained the conscious and subconscious mind. It sounds highly scientific, but he explained it in a way that was so easy to understand that I cannot help but share it:

I want you to imagine a big circle. In that circle, there is a line across the middle, dividing the circle in half. The circle represents the human mind. On one side of the line is your conscious mind, and on the other side is the subconscious mind. Allow me to explain what that means:

The subconscious mind is developed from when you are a baby. It takes care of all the stuff we do, but don't know we are doing. All the physiological functions of your body are controlled by the subconscious mind: heartbeat, circulation, digestion – everything. It is operating from the moment we are born, and we do not even know it. The subconscious is also the part of the brain that stores everything that we learn so that we can retrieve it whenever we need to. That is why we are not constantly thinking about every single thing we have ever learnt in school, yet we are able to recall much of it upon request. This also means that the way we think is all programmed into the subconscious mind – our habits, our beliefs, everything. The person we think we are, our personality, and our identity are all stored in the subconscious. We have no control over the environment we are born into, and yet we are a direct product of it simply through the way in which we store information.

At around the age of four, our conscious or 'thinking' mind is created. Now, we have the ability to accept or reject things. So, at four years old, you can decide what cookie you like, you can say yes or no, you can say you do not like broccoli or Brussels sprouts. However, your conscious mind is limited compared to the subconscious mind. This means that the subconscious will override the conscious mind. You will look for what you believe to be real and true from your subconscious via your conscious mind.

The line that separates the conscious mind from the subconscious mind is called the BS line. By that I do not mean what you probably think I mean – there's no need to swear! What I am talking about is the belief system line; it is what tells us if what we are currently learning in the conscious mind aligns with what we have already been taught to believe in the subconscious mind. For example, in your

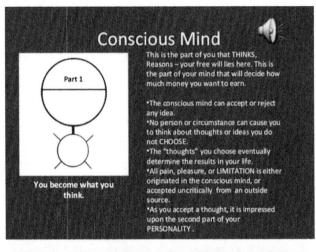

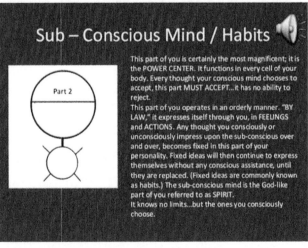

The pictures are from this website
https://www.slideshare.net/tommyhilcken/the-stickman

subconscious mind, you have a belief that pigs are pink. If I were to tell you that pigs were purple, that information would go into your conscious mind and then into the subconscious, past that BS line. Of course, the claim that pigs are purple does not match up with your current belief that pigs are pink, so your mind will be alerted to the fact that you have been given false information – you will automatically be distrustful.

All of your experiences, your beliefs, what you've been taught by your parents or those who raised you, are hard-wired into your subconscious even though you did not put them there. These beliefs may not even be serving you; they are simply what you have been taught. For this reason, it is important to understand how we remove those beliefs, and how we get past that belief system line so that we can create new beliefs that serve you.

How do we go about doing this? The answer is simple – through repetition. The more you say something, see it, hear it, do it, the more it becomes something that you believe. When you repeat something over and over again, it takes 21 days for it to become a new belief or habit. The more you do the thing, or tell it to yourself, the more you create it as a new belief. From this, it becomes easier to imagine how you can go from being in a place of 'I can't do this' to believing confidently in yourself through continuing to do the same thing. This can also work through repeating positive affirmations to yourself, telling yourself repeatedly that you can do it so that it becomes a belief that is stored in the subconscious mind.

Changing our beliefs and perceptions of who we think we are is also done through use of our senses – seeing, hearing, feeling, and doing. Seeing a YouTube video of how to do something, hearing a teacher explain it, doing the thing itself, and experiencing what it is like. When we tap into the senses, it gives us this incredible ability to create new beliefs and mindsets. If we can create a negative feeling about ourselves, for instance, if we wake up every morning and say, 'Life is bad, I can't do this', then the perception that is worked into the subconscious is that life is bad and we cannot do it.

But if we can convince ourselves of a negative truth, then the same must be true about positive truths. If we can convince ourselves that life is bad through repetition, we can convince ourselves that life is good through repetition as well. A belief is simply repetition of information. We have the power to create a whole new perception of the world and we have control over that perception. It does not mean we need the world to change, it means we need to change how we see the world.

Allow me to break this down further, into creating beliefs and habits:

Beliefs

What is a belief? A piece of information that has been instilled in us through repetition – that is all it is. We normally believe what we believe because we hear it from a source that we trust, like a parent or a close friend. We do not have any control over the beliefs instilled in us as children but we do have the power to change what they are today.

Here's the way I see it:

- If you believe you can, you're right

- If you believe you can't, you're also right

When you truly believe that you can do something, you will make it happen. It becomes a part of your reality. That is what a belief is. If you tell yourself enough times that you are going to do something, it becomes a permanent fixture in the mind. You have created a belief. The more you say something, the more you do it, hear it, the closer you are to making a new belief. The trouble is, most of the beliefs that control your life, were either created as a child or created by other people.

Here is the crazy part: you can override any belief you have that is not serving you, and you can create new ones. How cool is that? You can design a program in your mind that is going to give you the life that you want to live. You can create a perception of the world that only looks for the good. This is going to give you control over your life. A lot of people live with one view of the world forever, whether it serves them or not, simply because they do not know that they can change it. But there is no need to settle for the life you have been given. You have the ability to change the way you see the world and the way you see yourself simply through repetition of the information you wish to believe.

Habits

We are habitual creatures. 90% of the time we are running through the same things we always do on autopilot without even thinking. Have you ever driven to the shop and thought, 'I don't remember how I got here'? That is because when you do something over and over again, it becomes a habit and you can do it without even thinking. That is the power of the subconscious mind – we can do things without thinking.

However, just like our deeply ingrained beliefs, sometimes we cling on to habits that are not enhancing our lives or serving us. For example, we know we need to be healthier, and we know exactly how to do it but we don't do it. We know what exercises to do, we know what to eat but we don't do it. Why? Because our habits are so deeply ingrained within us that they start running our lives. The good news is, just like beliefs, our habits can be replaced. We can replace our bad habits with better ones – and it only takes 21 days to do so.

To remove a bad habit from your life, you need to replace it with another habit – a good habit. If you are a messy person and you want to be an organised person, then you need to clean and tidy the space around you for 21 days for it to become a habit. At this point, it becomes something you do without thinking, just like driving to the shop. This is why it's so important that we understand what our habits are, whether they are serving us, and how we can create new ones to replace them. This process will not work unless we do it every day without stopping.

It takes 21 days to create a new habit. That does not mean doing something once a week, it means doing it every single day without fail until you do not have to think about it anymore. It's like brushing your teeth, you have been doing it for so long that you don't even think about it anymore. That's how ingrained you want your new habits to be.

I POSSESS THE QUALITIES NEEDED TO BE EXTREMELY SUCCESSFUL.

Chapter 4: The Ego

The ego is a part of the mind that has been created throughout your life. It is demanding, primitive, and, ultimately, it wants you to be perfect. It worries about judgement, it is sensitive, and it craves approval from others and society as a whole. But your ego is not you. And in order to achieve true happiness, we must find a way to live without this need for validation. So how do we go about edging the ego to the side and learn to make a fool of ourselves, to express ourselves, to be vulnerable?

We all have an ego, we must accept this first. The best way to deal with the ego is to understand we are more powerful than it. We can think of the ego as a character within us but we should not allow it to be the driving force in our lives.

Dealing with the ego

Here is something for you to remember: you are a soul having a human experience, you are more than who you see in the mirror. You are a **soul** having a **human** experience. When you understand that, you realise that it is not in your best interest to be like everyone else. You do not need to accept external validation or prove yourself to people, you just need to be yourself. You cannot fail at being yourself.

But where does our sense of self come from in the first place? Our identities and the labels put on us by others are the ones we normally live by. Often, we go through life without really realising how much we are adhering to the rules and norms set by others. If we want to live the lives we want, however, we cannot afford to live by the standards of others. To live on our terms, we have to remove these identities that are placed on us by other people. You are unique and you are not meant to be in a box. Instead of allowing others to decide what kind of person you are, decide the characteristics that you want to have as a person and adhere to only those characteristics. Rid yourself of any other labels and be only the person you wish to be.

Allow me to use myself as an example. When I thought about the person I wanted to be, I thought about the heaviness of my past experiences and my fear and shyness around speaking up as a child. I thought about how great it would feel to be the kind of person who was not affected by any of that kind of stuff. The person who rose above everything to be their own person. So I wrote down: I am a free spirit. In doing this, I removed other identities from myself that had been put on me by society, my peers, my family. I stripped it back to the basics: I am a soul having a human experience. Once you know who you want to be, once you have that clear image of yourself, you are no longer limited by the expectations and labels of others.

You need to sell this story to yourself: you don't need to be anyone else or receive approval. You are the one who needs to validate yourself, it is not the job of anyone else. You only need your own approval.

When you understand this, it will be the moment you will really see that you are more than your ego. To live out your purpose in life, you need to be able to put the ego to the side, you need to let go of the fear of what others will say about you. I get that you are scared – your current identity is protected by your ego – but now it's time to assert your control. Say it out loud, 'I am in control'. And then say 'My "Why" is bigger than my fear of being judged'. These will be your mantras for letting go of the ego.

I want you to make a commitment to yourself that the fear of being judged will not hold you back anymore. Be vulnerable, speak your mind, use your voice – if you are judged, so be it. You do not need anyone's approval anymore. Set an example to those around you and around the world: it is okay to be you, it is okay to be judged, you cannot die from the judgement of others. This is your freedom we are talking about, and you are claiming it.

Think of it this way: we are not born with shame. We are not born with embarrassment. We are not born with fear of judgement from others. When you were a baby you did not care about anything you did, you did not think about judgement or what others thought of you, you were in the moment. Then you grew up and you took on the shame that society wanted to place on you, so you began to fear the judgement of others. The best-kept secret of life that I have found so far is that you do not *have* to carry that shame around with you. If you overcome the fear of judgement, if you overcome that ego, your best life is waiting for you on the other side.

You are in control of the ego. You have the power. The more you tell these things to yourself through affirmations, the closer you become to being the person you want to be.

Repeat after me:

I am more than my ego

I do not care about being judged

I cannot fail at being myself

Create these beliefs within yourself by repeating them every single day.

The importance of a morning routine:

I cannot stress enough how much setting aside time at the beginning of the day to practice what I had learnt helped me in my journey.

Everything you have read so far: your 'Why', your mindset, knowing your goals and who you want to be, are all leading up to eventually taking action.

I started this routine for my mornings when I was reprogramming my mind to create the habits and beliefs that I knew I needed to change my life. It is a four-part process:

1. Your 'Why'	We have been over how to emotionally connect with your 'Why', but now it is time to learn how to use it to make your life better. Using your 'Why' in a morning routine requires you connecting not only your mind and emotions to it but your physiology too. Write down your 'Why' and put it on your bedroom wall. Get up in the morning, stand tall with your feet apart and chin up. Put your hands on your heart and say out loud why you need to do this. Feel your heart pumping and connect with the energy behind your reason. You are now physically embodying your 'Why'. This is going to help keep it at the forefront of your mind and allow you to overcome the challenges you're faced with..
2. Gratitude	Gratitude is one of the most important things you should do in the morning. Most people wake up, put the news on and feed their mind with all of that negativity and then they expect to have a positive day. Imagine, if you were to wake up and to focus on those things you are grateful for. The things that money can't buy and the things we sometimes take for granted like our family or the clean water that comes out of your taps. You see, what you focus on is what you attract more of. Did you know, that it's impossible to be down and grateful at the same time? Write down five things that you are truly grateful for, that if you were to think about those things now, they would make you emotional. This, my friend, is the secret to happiness. Read them every single morning after your 'Why'.
3. Affirmation	An affirmation is saying a statement repeatedly until it becomes a new belief. The subconscious mind doesn't work through logic, it works by repetition. So if you tell yourself something over and over again, it then becomes a belief. For example, most people fail because of a negative affirmation such as 'I'm not good enough'. Maybe you've said this before. It's about having self-awareness of the beliefs you have that limit you, so that you can override and replace them. Your subconscious mind is always on record and it doesn't care whether what you're saying is negative or positive, it listens. For example, you may have a current belief that you are shy and you would like to be more confident. One of your morning affirmations could be, 'I am confident'. The repetition of this daily will then replace 'I am shy' with 'I am confident'.

3. Affirmation	Understanding the limiting beliefs you have about yourself is essential in order that you can remove the negative things you say to yourself and replace them with positive affirmations. You can apply this to all areas of your beliefs and life including personal development, relationships and even your financial situation. Write down a minimum of five affirmations and repeat these every morning. Place them all around your home where you will see them constantly...
4. Visualisation	I want you to see yourself like an architect – you don't see builders just putting some bricks together and then making a house. The architect's job is to create a design that is so precise that the house ends up looking exactly like the design, brick for brick. We must see it in our mind, long before we achieve it. The mind can't determine the difference between what is real and what is imagined so if you can visualise the person that you want to become and you picture yourself stepping into that more confident self, feeling how it feels to be that person, and what it's like to walk in their shoes, then sooner or later, you will become that person in reality. Your mind will have created the beliefs and the identities to become that person. What I mean by that person is the the best version of you. So I want you to get yourself a cork board and separate it into four different sections: personal goals, financial goals, contribution and a final category of your choosing. Personal goals consists of the traits of the person you want to become whether that's loving yourself more or maybe being more confident, financial goals could be the amount of money you want to earn or the house you want you and your family to live in, contribution consists of ways in which you want to help other people and the final category is something you choose for yourself. Write down and get pictures to represent all of your goals and pin them onto your cork board. During this final step of your daily routine, stand in front of your vision board and step into that new life. Imagine how it is going to feel when you achieve those goals and the person that you will become. This is something you have to do every single day to make your vision become a reality.

Throughout the morning routine, you should also try taking notes in this gratitude journal:

5 things I am most grateful for:
    1.
    2.
    3.
    4.
    5.

Name 3 great funny memories that have happened in your life
    1.
    2.
    3.

What makes me feel most happy?

What in my life excites me?

What in my life do I forgive myself for?

What am I trying to achieve before I die?

I AM LIVING IN
AN ENVIRONMENT THAT
SUPPORTS MY MENTAL,
EMOTIONAL AND SPIRITUAL
WELL BEING.

_____

Chapter 5: Your Environment

They say we are a product of our environment. How true is that?

It is so important that we become aware of our surroundings, because they influence who we are, our beliefs, and our identities. If you want to become the best version of yourself, then it is imperative that you create the right environment for that version of you to thrive. We know that

Illustration: Edie.net

we cannot control the outside world; our brains are constantly on overload from all of the outside information that we have to process every day. We walk down the street and we see photographs of models posing in expensive brands, telling us that we are not good enough and that we need to buy the products to be worthy. That is how marketing works. They want us to believe that we need that product so that they can make sales. But this results in all of us living in an environment where we are told we are unworthy every single day; it is not conducive to a positive mindset.

But the great thing about your environment that no one ever tells you is that we can also make it work to our advantage. If we surround ourselves with the right information, then we can create that positive environment in our own household and therefore a positive mindset.

Begin with your bedroom. Make your bedroom a growth environment. For example, what I did at the start of my journey was to put affirmations all over my bathroom and bedroom along with my

'Why', gratitude list and vision board so that I was surrounded by the life I wanted to live. This is your space, and you have complete control over how it makes you feel. Having all of this around you is going to remind you of the journey you are on. Even when you are not paying attention to them, even when you are not reading them out loud, the messages are still getting into your subconscious, just like the billboard advertisements were. Then, a few times a day, say the affirmations out loud too, and embody the emotions so they can create beliefs.

The next step is the social environment that you are in. Jim Rohn famously said that you are the average of the five people you surround yourself with. By this, he means that the people you choose to have around you in life are either lifting your life up or bringing your life down. These people are either bringing you closer towards your goals or taking you further away from them. This is a hard part of the journey, but you need to ask yourself, 'Should these people be in my life?' Are they helping you grow, are they helping you achieve your goals? Do they encourage you to do more rather than less? Do they push you to work harder and be a better version of yourself? Do they also want the best for their own lives? If you are around people who are going where you want to go, then that rubs off on you. Surround yourself with people doing the things you want to do, the people who you know will be a great influence on your journey. Find those who lift you and help you be better. It is so important to actively evaluate who you have in your life. If they do not have the same goals as you, then their advice is not always going to be the best for you; only you can know what is best for your journey. Surrounding yourself with the right people is a big part of how you see the world – the subconscious mind is always open and taking everything in, even when we are not aware of it.

I TAKE ACTION WITHOUT
DOUBT WHEN A NEW IDEA
COMES TO ME.

_____

Chapter 6: Taking Action

I have now given you most of the ingredients that I believe you need to change your life. We have talked through the 'Why', the mindset, the importance of a great morning routine, speaking affirmations, learning new habits and beliefs, and the importance of our environment. Now, I am going to talk you through the most crucial ingredient of the recipe: Action.

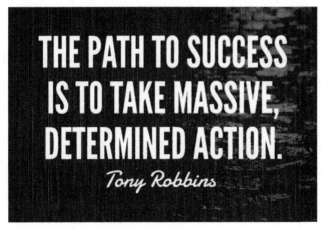

Illustration: https://yourpositiveoasis.com/

Writing down your morning routine, affirmations, gratitude, your 'Why', your vision of who you want to be, and your environment – these are only the set-up process that leads you to the crucial moment where you can either choose to follow through or to abandon all that you have learnt. This is the vital point: we have to get to work.

How do we take action? I am going to talk you through it:

First, you have to put your affirmations into physical action. You now know who you want to become and all of that person's characteristics, now all that is left is to become that person. I will use the confidence example again: if you want to be more confident, you have got to walk confidently. Lift your shoulders back, keep your chin up.

The action is everything, it is not enough to simply write down what you want; you have to physically do it. Yes, you are going to have to come out of your comfort zone – becoming the person you want to be is not done by staying where you are comfortable.

But whatever it is that you think you cannot do – journaling on social media, public speaking, interviewing, writing, whatever it is – you just have to do it. You might think you can't, but that is only because you haven't done it before. Thinking that you can't, simply because you haven't, is a limiting belief perpetuated by the ego, and it is not a mindset that you have to keep. Becoming comfortable in an uncomfortable situation is the absolute key to growth. So go out and make a fool of yourself, be embarrassed, be uncomfortable and vulnerable, and let that become the new norm. Stop caring what others think of you and enjoy the freedom that it gives you to not care. Beyond the comfort zone is the learning zone, which is uncomfortable and hard, but beyond the learning zone is the growth zone – and that is where the real magic happens. I would say 1 in 10 people take action – make sure you are that one person. You have been ready to change your life for a long time and keep putting it off or making excuses but now is your time.

This is the technique I used when I wanted to be confident speaking on stage. I will admit, I did it in an extreme way, but it worked. I was so scared of failing and what others thought of me, and I knew that unless I learnt not to care, it would only hold me back. So I decided not to let that happen. One day, I walked into a fancy restaurant, and I decided that this was the perfect place to get out of my comfort zone. I decided that, in the middle of this restaurant, I was going to start singing. I was terrified, but I knew that it would teach me a valuable lesson that I think we all need to learn: that I couldn't die from people judging me. Nothing bad could happen because of someone else's opinion of me. So I did it, I sang in the restaurant; I didn't even know the lyrics to the song I was singing, but I did it anyway. I could feel people judging me, which was painful at first, but when I walked outside again, I felt so elated that I punched the air. I did it, I did not die, nothing bad happened at all. This taught me the value of learning to be comfortable in uncomfortable situations and the more I did things like this, the easier it became for me.

Use the 21 day process to track your progression from the comfort zone to the Growth Zone. You can change anything in your life in 21 days. Journal your progress for the entire 21 days, become self-aware, and hold yourself to the highest level of accountability. Say your affirmations throughout the day, repeat them until they become so deeply embedded in your brain that you cannot help but believe them. Take time each day to learn about personal growth and mindset, and set yourself a challenge of applying that information at least once throughout the day. At night, take time for self-reflection and write down how you applied the information you learnt. Write down three things you improved on today and three more that you can improve for tomorrow. This is how we track growth – through daily consistent actions.

I AM COURAGEOUS AND
I STAND UP FOR MYSELF.

———————

Chapter 7:
The Six Principles of Success

Know Your Worth

Define your identity and realise your standards in every aspect of your life. Know that you deserve better than what you have right now, and know that you can have better, too. Once we know that we deserve better, we are able to put everything into getting there.

'When your self-worth goes up, your net worth goes up with it' – *Mark Victor Hansen*

Know Your 'Why'

Develop a reason for pursuing your dream, a 'Why' that is so emotional that it will get you up before your alarm clock. This is the fuel to our determination. The bigger the 'Why', the smaller the obstacles.

'When you know your WHY, you can endure any HOW.' – *Viktor Frankl*

Giving Back

The act of giving is a feeling like no other. If you make your purpose in life about what you can do for others rather than what you can do for yourself, then you will meet your goals so much faster.

Knowing that others are depending on you reaching your goals gives you a larger purpose, and therefore a better chance of achieving what you want.

'You can have everything you want in life if you just help enough people get what they want' – *Jim Rohn*

Lose the Fear of Being Judged

Life is about expressing who you are, not impressing people. Once you lose the fear of being judged, you will be able to express yourself and be the real you all the time. Other people will always have opinions about you, and they are entitled to those, but it should not define how you feel about yourself.

'You have no responsibility to live up to what other people think you ought to accomplish. I have no responsibility to be like they expect me to be. It's their mistake, not my failing' – *Richard P. Feynman*

Gratitude

Once you master gratitude, you will become more emotionally intelligent. It is impossible to be down and grateful at the same time.

'Acknowledging the good that you already have in your life is the foundation for all abundance' – *Eckhart Tolle*

Destination

Knowing exactly what you want in life is vital. It gives you direction and purpose. The majority of people are lost when it comes to goals and

aspirations because they do not know their purpose. The secret is to know exactly what you are
moving towards, and move towards it at any cost.

'Setting goals is the first step in turning the invisible
into the visible' – *Tony Robbins*

These are the principles of success that I live by.
Using these, I have paved the way for my own
success and the success of many others. These
principles are the building blocks; if you use all of
them correctly, you will build a successful life for
yourself. Once you learn the art of being yourself,
you will realise your power and that you can't fail
being you.

TODAY I ABANDON MY OLD HABITS AND TAKE UP NEW, MORE POSITIVE ONES.

————————

Chapter 8: The 21 Day Mind and Body Program

It is time to put everything we have learnt into practice.

Before you even begin, you are prepared, you have your morning routine written down, you have it in a place where you're going to see it every morning, you have your 'Why' mission statement to emotionally connect you to why you're doing this so that you don't give up, you've got your gratitude list with the things you're grateful for. You know the person you want to become. Anything you do not like about yourself can be removed. Once you make these changes and repeat them for 21 days, they will become habitual. Record your journey, either on social media (use #gotthismovement) or privately, in order to hold yourself accountable. Reach out to me on social media at Warren Inspire Ryan and let me know you are starting this journey. This is the thing in life that is worth showing up for – your development and growth to become the person you want to be is worth dedicating your energy to. There will be good days, and there will be bad days, and there will be days where the last thing you feel like doing is showing up for yourself. But regardless of that, showing up for yourself is exactly what you are going to do.

Through your journey, you are going to get a sense of contribution as well, which is the most valuable currency there is. People are going to tell you how you have inspired them, and that feeling is out of this world. You'll be living a life of purpose, a life dedicated to seeking the truth, to finding yourself, to creating yourself, and contributing to a greater cause. That is a life worth living.

I am your biggest supporter, I want you to win. I got this. You got this. We got this.

I ACKNOWLEDGE MY OWN
SELF-WORTH;
MY CONFIDENCE IS
SOARING.

You finished the book, which means that you fulfilled your commitment to yourself, but the journey does not end here. In fact, it is only just beginning.

For more information about the 21 day course, including a free audio, head over to **www.gotthismovement.com.**

About the Author:

Warren Inspire Ryan is an international speaker and founder of the Got This Movement, who has impacted the lives of thousands of people around the world by helping them find their voice.

Warren has created the rapidly growing Got This Movement which is an online platform that provides all the resources to thrive in wellbeing, health and fitness, and business. He has hosted events, retreats, and workshops, teaching the methods within this book.

When he isn't traveling the world speaking, Warren likes to spend time with his family: Rosie, son Noah, daughter Mila, and step-son Ezra. This work wouldn't have been completed without his fiancée, Rosie, who supported Warren at his lowest point in this life.

A huge shout out to the book launch team:

Lesley Tucker

Nicole Tatum

Serena Marie Heath

Paula Maragh

Samantha Ollewagen

Zak Haque

Linda Easto

Jo Richardson

Annalaura Serpico

Keith Gray

Rosie Leach

Lucy Marsh

Chloe Ryan

Printed in Great Britain
by Amazon

60313666R00051